ARTIFICIAL LIFE

Michael Gessner

BlazeVOX [books]

Buffalo, New York

ISBN: 9781935402299
Library of Congress Control Number: 2009925612

BlazeVOX [books]
14 Tremaine Ave
Kenmore, NY 14217

Editor@blazevox.org

publisher of weird little books

BlazeVOX [books]

blazevox.org

2   4   6   8   0   9   7   5   3   1

B   X

Grateful acknowledgment is made to those publications in which
some of these poems first appeared:

10 X 3: "Talk," (2008 Pushcart Prize nomination,) "Salton Sea," "Departure,"
   "The Sublime," "Utility," "Flyleaf," "Best Said"
Atticus Review: "Minor Figures"
The Aurorean: "Pregnant Girl on The Genesee River Bridge"
Buffalo Spree Magazine: "The Carmine Cycle," "Smoke," "Sonora Saying,"
   "Urban Development"
Eclipse: "Promiscuity," "Washing before Sex"
Oxford Magazine: (reprinted in *Dog Music*, St. Martin's Press,)
   "Lines on a Dog's Face"
Poem: (University of Alabama Press,) "Sunday Picnic"
Sycamore Review: (Purdue University,) "The Tropic Gardens of St. Gallen"

CONTENTS

ARTIFICIAL LIFE

TALK

We talk it out whenever
we are alone, or when we are not,
when we are about to do it,
right before we pull out
the old lie again,
shake it off to show the crowd,
say in the boardroom when presenting
our case before the city council,
whenever we are about to move
forward we must talk about it first.
Our adversaries will not complain
as much if we repeat them,
as if we are actually considering
what they are saying.

'Talk about it and you will feel
better,' the accused is told,
and tho' this may be so, what we
really want to know is the gossip,
'tell us the whole story,' we say pulling
the chair closer to the speaker,
to the other made vulnerable,
exposed, as we know ourselves
to have been, and all the talk
in the world cannot put it right,
tho' we continue to search
for the perfect story of ourselves,
the one we can wrap around
our bodies, lie down, live inside.

When we talk the small talk
about the weather, as if we ourselves
are warm, or cold, we also talk
the talk of avoidance, 'I love to hear
you talk,' she said staring into his eyes,
hearing nothing. Table talk, the talking
we do on our night out on the town,
at the booth reserved in the back,
in a semi-circle of red velvet
curtains, where we first whispered
our plans and our longings
that did nothing but put us
in our place, the place we have
sought all our lives.

We promise to move on
before we talk it to death,
in the bedroom we make sure
the other agrees
to the arrangement, so it will
all go well, as planned,
so there won't be any misgivings,
regrets, even tho' there are always
regrets, even if they are
small and fleeting.
And later, if we have problems,
a bad settlement, unreasonable demands
on our lives, we talk it over.
It gives us time, sympathy,

maybe some options. We talk late
into the night, sometimes talk
until we are exhausted, what we
will do with the mortgage, our loved ones,
the right to die. The distraught lover
goes on until he is talked out.
The guy on the ledge who might be
one-in-the-same is talked down.
And should we say we have nothing
left to give, we may be accused
of poor talk, or if talk is used
as a substitute for an expected outcome
that does not occur, words instead of deeds
the poets know talk is cheap.

Even the gift of gab is not
immune from this accusation,
as if we could not read
ourselves in someone else's saying,
as if we could not find ourselves,
the shape of our soul, in talk.
'What could we say,' they said
after the Basilica of St. Francis collapsed
from an earthquake. Then the talk began
once again, quietly, as if they should not be
talking at all about rebuilding,
'Let's talk it up. We will rebuild
the Basicila,' they said when they were
rebuilding the holy temple of talk.

Talking in circles
we are circles of talk,
the talking of taking ideas
away from their home
in the staid grotto of rumination
where those of us familiar
with the settings of antiquities loiter,
and placing them on board
one of the Voyagers, we are talk,
all talk, the talk of the town, incessant
talk, double talk, we talk on waking
to discuss the day, we talk it through
talk and talk until we are blue
in the face.

CASES

A Cosmography
for Danaé

Location is everything.

The order of worlds

is as seafoam & as infinite   today

in unison their identity is of the mass & not the cell,

not the cell as in cacophony, ascent, hiddenness   the realtors are on

from all others   the prowl

thus beauty finds virtue.

                                                          & must be

                                                          left on the streets

                                                          where they cannot find

                                                          themselves

& when in winter I look on the one

 field of snow, those paratactic cones

commingling from the narrow now   vices   like voices

or in the ascent, my body, your body,   in a braid

dissolving into smaller & smaller mounds

of color or white puffs of air

rolling overhead   a variation

on the horizons   of galactic dust

stories of space   in cells

reforming themselves

& in rheotaxis   & here we are

            swarms   flocks schools clutches

      & finally space said,   always two things,

      my children have found themselves—

      it is my double   what we are

            in the dormer   & what we are not

& there tucked behind the Dali painting

on the wall down the hallway

is the one voice of the match stick girl   a single voice per body,

                                    the poet's allowance

      E   I   D   O   L   A   N   I   A

ii Cuttings & Nets

The peripheries share their elements

in lines crossing   the gangplanks of displacement

over others or nudging up   wherein turnstiles

against themselves   all chrome & glistening

as if to imitate an exchange   turn & re-turn

     or play

iii The Grand Palace   & the youth hostel

     of Fraudulence   with graffiti

which is everywhere,   there/their

so much so that the locus

needs not be re-created,

the cells of red brick, a house   for sale or lease

the cells of the human heart,   a homebody

pixels of fractal symmetries

& in the Euclidian diatrix that surrounds

the interiors of spheres   o hope

     my hope, your hope,

in the envelope on my desk

the girl had left a note:

'I don't know if you received this

[email] so I made a copy.

You signed 'Michael'. I could never

call you that, so never ask.

And as far as our meeting goes,

I can't get away until next Thursday.

My father is ill

and I am expected back

home. After that we will just have to cancel all

other commitments. Arrangements must be made.

Last night, before I went to sleep, I was

remembering you, and then I could not

remember your face. It terrified me.

      Forever & Always,

          Rachel Frances

be available, take

that course in semiotics,

take earthly vestments

& clothe your invisible self,

walk with me

through the garden
of
kitsch & kunst

in the operation

of cones

spinning & fluorescent

centrifuge inside

a box

you wore your tiny bits of body glitter

                         she said & about the things

                         that seemed to float above us

                         & descend when we do not

                         expect them

micas & schools of mirrors

> "We imagine we are observed and of concern to someone."

> —Czeslaw Milosz, *Road-Side Dog*

iv Narrative Acts

There are events that remain untainted, or purified, by language, and at the
same time, known by it. While these remain apart from, and are in every
respect, 'mindless' of story structure, or of anything we may understand as
'linguistic' in nature, they are nonetheless engaged in it, [in the structure of
an event, we might call story,] and because of our ability to talk about them
in descriptions of their operations. These events are metamythic, and speak
directly to experience from experience of the natural world. However we
may clothe them in myth, they operate independently. If the narrative is
reduced to its constituents, we are likely to find actors, (or a thing that
interacts with another—characters, objects, settings—*et. al.*,) a *locus*,
(place or setting,) conflicts, goals, and resolutions. These may appear
singly, say as in a sentence, ('The rock tumbled down the cliff and flattened
the hut,') or in multiples, ('The rocks tumbled down the cliff and flattened
the village', or 'The rocks pried loose by the angered enemy, were sent down
 the mountainside to crush the villagers'. Each (of the six above named
constituents,) may function as an agent, or agents of the other, and in effect,
the whole of the narrative, or for that matter, *any* narrative. Thus, & likewise,
a narrative grammar. If we include the description of static things, there
is no thing outside of it. Cases in hand. The meaning of anything that is
to have meaning.

There is only the grammar of action   and the grammar of inaction.

German ornithologists recently recorded common jays
& starlings replicating the ringtones of cell phones in Tuebingen.
It seems birds indigenous to the countryside have come to the
cities in growing numbers in search of a convenient source of
food left by humans in an increasingly affluent, throw-away
culture, and have found modern technology at its most enchanting
& seductive.

The Australian lyrebird, so named for the cartilage that helps display
the (almost flagrant) fan of tail feathers shaped like a Grecian lyre,
imitates the Kookaburra with such accuracy it elicits kindred
responses. The lyrebird's repertoire includes just about anything
that can produce audible sound waves: car alarms, chainsaws,
trains, even the clicking of a camera shutter. Its reproductions
are so precise, the human ear cannot detect the difference between
the sound it makes of the chainsaw, for example, and the real thing.

entry: . . . Notes on the Art of Imitation . . .

As for the grammar of inaction there is this: the patch of sunlight

                on the study floor.

            a rock   a hut   a village/villager

                    cliffs

Other events that may be related by way of the narrative are
also factual in the operations of the natural world:

Genine Lentine in an interview with Stanley Kunitz,
(*American Poetry Review*, May/June 2006: v.35:3,)
discussed the centenarian's affection for gardening,
and at one point, noted she had observed grasshoppers
copulate for 45 minutes, and snails, for hours.

In contrast to snails, I have observed mourning doves
land on my garden gate and go through their mating ritual.
After a kind of awkward pecking motion, like Europeans
who kiss one side of the cheek then the other, but seem to
be pretending—Hollywood air kisses—there is a fluttering
of wings in which the male mounts the back of the female, and
the event occurs. This entire process takes, at most, 20 seconds.

On the animal channel, I have seen a silverback gorilla pull
a female over to him with one arm, adjust himself, followed
by a brief shudder, and return to munching foliage, as does the female.

They seem to be unaware that anything had ever occurred.

        A case of involuntary copulation. *Natura fabula.*

  It is in the course. It is not outside the course. That is not language.

  Somewhere it is market day.

  Property is property.   Call it what you will.

  Multiple listings, open houses.

  There are only re-formations   (all new things cannot be said
                                           to have had pre-existing
                                           particles or fragments
                                           that have not merged with
                                           an unknown)

               & some beyond recognition

as a perfect sphere of space   one

                        might say

imagination   has no law but forms,
                            no forms, but energy,
                            no shapes but those of energy
                            & the assumptions of energy
o mammatus clouds   those heavy matrons of fecundity

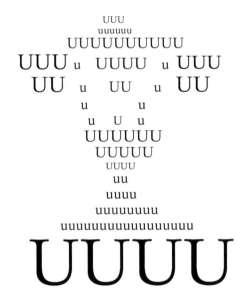

Most corpulent breasts of rare sky & thus u

are that sign

(& intersection)

Celestial Megapolae

The Chimerae are in the banks. Continent islands or island continents.

Liminals on the colonials   newly listed
                                                               addresses

ghost corpses

seafoam cupped in the hand   by the human hand

v Torque

Solar flares   microwaves

heat distorts the horizon   in waves

effusions that seem sporadic

& must be due to long sessions   of planning

        or some eruption

        that had something,   spun out

an effusion against the sky   against a dark night

                        the darkest night

                        when no thing could

        the boy Perseus   imagine itself or any   in the sea-tossed box

        & the marriage   of Andromeda

                            other thing

& I called out, saying, Juan, San Juan where is my lover . . .

in absence of the body, I have kissed corpses, my corpse, your corpse,

& there was no answer & still I called until I could no longer speak, &

there was silence. In the silence I imagined stillness. Though there was never

stillness, not in anything among the cells and the clusters of cells, never

```
            u
           UU
          UUUU
         UUUUUU
       UUUUUUUU
     UUUUUUUUUUUU
       UUUUUUUUU
        UUUUUU
         UUUU
          UU
           U
```

if only u were the shape of a porous crystal & thus unique, & say, uvular, bulky,

    & light in ur bulkiness
           & bulky in ur lightness,

great attractors have found homes in the simplest forms,

the illusion that arises in the spray of water, the child who cannot

speak, the flower tucked away from any observer, these have

the knowledge of the hydraulics of sunlight.

                                                    Recesses.

Plate techtonics operate in their disruption/ commissures,

lumpy ridges on the hills of the painted desert & the surface of the

cortex are from the same reason.

                                                    absence

        Who said   the scene was full

        the night air   of spring

        was reorganized   with the crushed offering

                        of Boswellia

                            &

                        Commiphora

    & unknown   outside

                    the choking
                    sulfur of panic

    0   0

            (diatom in service of the organelle)

& that it was for other structures going their ways at once

so dimension consumes the perspective of the spot (0)

like an implosion of dust or tide—the Red Sea—going backward

& thus rearranging the case & the relative status of a) interventions,

b) shape, size, & c) what we have not yet come to

> (what has pre-existed us & what
> is with us now cannot complete
> itself with knowing & yet cannot
> be exclusive)

vi Olfactorium

      the mornings of lavender   in a new subdivision

           the re-loclation
           when births are

      conducted like an appraisal

   & attractive   like the first suggestion

   of floating a loan

      in those concessions   of seafoam

   & (thus) the greasy communal smells of subways after working hours

the smell of history in wet straw,
the smell of anger in the snout, full of metal filings,
or condemnation, steel on steel,
& later, lavender, or guilt's residue

burnt cherry

zeal	flint (or lightning before it strikes)
charity	pollens released with breeze's breath
moderation	ozone/the odor of vacuity
meekness	wet loam/ yeast
generosity	the open field that asks nothing
humility	the saffron in the air at the sun's going & coming
chastity	starched linen

on a cold morning airwaves commingle; the hounds are

confused, start off on trails that soon turn into other properties

Lust in spotted tights dances
over the tables of fat & gold,
pride & indolence, pirouettes over envy
sulking, paralyzed in a corner to bring
them all, every one, to its purpose
until proud Wrath (wrapped in a tux)
takes revenge with a chromium
mallet & the crowd applauds enthusiastically
so they are no longer distracted & may return
to their pursuits.

Note: Lust may be replaced by any other figure, (gluttony, greed, sloth, envy, wrath, vanity,) & operate as an agent. Say, greed, for example, could appear as a figure in Klimt:

> In her golden skirt with golden coins dangling
> Danaé dances the dance of the bee
> in the house of mirth & in the house of the agonies,
> over the tables of sloth & envy,
> the beds of sex & the table of mirrors, pirouettes over anger
> sulking in a soiled tux in the corner until
> the fat creature rises up to consume
> the gold girl & the crowd approves enthusiastically
> so they are no longer distracted by greed & may return
> to their pursuits.

The block is full of double-agents.

identical twins

counter-operatives

fragments kiss (as)

sex & greed

marbles click

chrome balls in the perpetual motion display

You dream in the joyless wood
In the night nailed in bronze,
In the blue dark you lie still & shine.

—Simonides

26

DANAÉ

Love had a difficult birth.

The old godhead had seen once more
beauty beyond beauty
September's gold bangle
in daisy-particled light
pollen from swollen anthers
like yellow semen dried out,
left too long in the sack,
an errant god's basket of sunlight,
the gold foil in a variation then,
as if the brass tower was not
prophetic, & the washing
down & down in gold showers,
raising the roof & the glimpse of her
& the boy in the box, what was risked for love
would never have occurred without hard cash,
money in the blood, shining
in her hair, all red & curled
around her leg curled in coitus
curled up like a fetal-adult,
the thigh with splotches
of gold, rose & saffron, translucencies
snatched from the Orion nebulae
all awash in the taunting speckled night,
turned up on her side, so it would
course through her, money running
through the veins of galactic clouds,
a gamble with eyes pinched tight
in heavenly torment
& turning colors, like body glitter
as though glittering was the thing itself,

Legenda Aurea, this
more than any other is
the central image
of the species, its *raison d'être*.

The sun set. It set itself down
between the two earthly mounds
& for this blind act I would be broke,
rocking myself to sleep in the universe of alleys,
airless & dim, with the artificial light
of a strange moon.

vii Agents of Operation

    a refuge for the homeless

                        mortuus ut orbis terrarum

the grammar of inaction hangs around like lavender in the morning . . .

  I shut my eyes   & I shut yours

  shut, a shutter of a mechanical lens

  a click or kiss,   & shut also

  & simultaneously   the polyverse,

                                flexivervse

  Master Locus   metaverse

    embracing absence   silicone on the skin

                            ferromagnetic displacement

by Van der Waals force

the envelope girl   whenever we met

distracted in the place

of the second-self

& this   there is this

notes of woodworm

                                     re-turn

re-turning   as we have been

returning

to the presence   that has clung   about us

                                     that cannot speak

for itself

& would never care to be

spoken for   by any other

                                     & yet insists on this
                                     presentation of cases
                                     & agents.

ARTIFICIAL LIFE

All performances today have been cancelled.

Make no mistake. There must be nothing
out of the ordinary, it's been posted,
no marching, we must stand fast.
The myth of the exploding star
and the next extinction have been
put on hold wherever you are
it too has been, innocence and the isolation
of the justice gene, the paper cut-out
on Valentine's Day underscoring
the shadowy lattice and blue thatch
that came with the biothermal work,
day labor grinding away again
without the special knowledge of anyone
not even the curators of armies
like the pencil sketches they made
of dark figures hiding in cellars,
no one in particular, going where they are
going, and the part-time return, agitated
about the revisions, the supreme biological
auction and the disagreeing classes of thought,
the grumbling forces, but they've been
shut down, as we speak, even the factories
across the street have closed for the day
until we get it straight, which cannot occur
because of all the new business coming to the valley
and all the others who remain uninformed.

NOT ABOUT THIS

It is not about the classic rivers
of mythology, not about Acheron,
river of woe with its lines of unemployed
holding their migraines in their hands.

Or Cocytus, river of lamentation
where the elderly have gone
to grieve their condition.

It cannot be this.

Not the river of fire,
the lava flowing from another volcanic shudder
into the homes of the living & the dead,
& into the stories of new generations.

For these are byproducts,

shining as they are—

It is not about the river of forgetfulness,
inviting as the night visits the tortured mind.
No, not this, or the waters of hate
& the butchered bodies stacked along shorelines
& the lost women trying to find their sons,

or the river of return,

not the red river of consolation
wound about the heart
& through the vineyards,
or how our loves came to be,
then left us again to ourselves.

It is not about the oldest & saddest river,
the river of time, with flashes of metallic film
sliding by gathering momentum,
& the surfaces of faces,
the faces of phantoms,
(I have seen myself among them.)

It cannot be about classical dramaturgy,
or if it is, it is the dramaturgy of celestial mechanics,
the giant narrative of everything,
the source of energy (& its forms)
crunching itself out through the heavens.

PROMISCUITY

The customer does not consider
the other customers
who have been here.

Even if it were possible
it would only confuse the mission
of the mind

which, at the moment, is being
serviced by twin sisters
who often perform in tandem.

They are the darlings
of the establishment
and are confident

of this. After all,
he is paying
for clarity,

not peace of mind,
not a day at the beach
with sand in the sandwiches.

The customer
also has a double
who sits in the lobby

and cannot come in
despite the best efforts
of the management.

He is trying to live
with order and restraint,
for a purpose beyond

his own and finding it
difficult. The twins
are amused.

They offer to help
and are refused
which embarrasses

the customer—
and though he does not understand
where he has been—

knows too well
his confusion before
and after these things.

AT THE NURSES' STATION
      IN THE HOSPITAL
            OF
   THE INCARNATE WORD

Here they come again. The halls buzz
with lights & motors. It never ceases.
They are formulating hypotheses
A, B, C, D, & so on. A series of maybes
blinking on & off all over the city
& the cities blink too, like civilizations.

When it is quiet, it gets serious.
The fellow across the hall
is so pale he's about to dissolve
so they've strapped him to a gurney,
taken him to the roof. It was necessary
to revive him. Everyone agreed.

The transplantation team argues
in the empty room. They want the remains.
The text will become someone else's
rumor, a biography in the lobby
of enthusiasm. The chief resident
has the situation in hand.

As for the pale fellow on the roof,
the old man who thought his soul
would turn into a star was convinced
otherwise by a confident night nurse.
This took weeks, whispering to him
when he was at his worst. Finally

he agreed with a cough. It was necessary
to do this before he died. The remainder
of the family refused to view the corpse.
The team met again, as usual
over coffee, some small talk, but this
is where the action begins.

There are new arrivals. A transit accident.
A series of rooms must be assigned,
a suite for history & memory, & others.
The hemorrhaging must cease before anything
can be done for Patient X , but this may not be
so important after all, because the emergency

room has been invaded by a group of advanced
asthmatics from across town. They recite
an eviction notice with the certainty
of a new culture & move with one body
to the lobby calling for the chief
resident up on the roof.

A NATURAL HISTORY OF DREAD

OR

THE ENTIRELY GREEN AVATARS

    of ambition are busy again chewing away
at the brainstem of the subject, even in light sleep
they remain conversant, gnawing at themselves
as if they were the only ones left alive.

    Meanwhile, morning comes, the day
drawls on, raining & the rain is busy also,
experiencing its own perfection which causes more
havoc among the green avatars.

    The subject nods, exhausted,
drowses off, his head jerks
back, connected to the invisible cord of terror
yanked by the incomplete life,
the fear of the unfinished

    work. Or worse. It is an announcement
screaming awake, sharp as a needle
on a nerve in the mouth of the human to say
that the Great Activity is having another Moment,

    a paroxysm of plenitude,
like the last death when the subject swam
out of the world of water in a similar fit, it is another
house call from the science of the possible

    to move to a concurrent reality
through one of being's invisible & impossible doors
screaming, he demands they leave & they sometimes do
as though they are weary also

of transforming themselves to the contours of thought
or necessity—of trying too long to stabilize
transient images against accelerating time, tired
from thinking in multiples

they curl in dormant corners
so there remains only the sound
& the shape of the sound,
the rainwater falling on terraces.

COMMENTARY ON MULTIPLE SYSTEMS

What brought them here was essential
as the variations of opinions themselves,
as chaos & harmony working through other lives
in distant regions at once & also in classes
of this time, in salons with walls
of metallic leaf, thin iridescent lavas
from deposits of common speech. They advance.

Near a parked car an argument breaks out
as others gather in the public park, an affair
under the moon my neighbor admires the iris garden
& for the present forgives loss & extravagance
in bubbling pools, in the cause of the general course
it is the night of the one shooting star.
The sky is clear as gratitude.

The spectacular, sought by a diverse group has broken
off from the party on the next block to form its own,
a commotion coming down my street, the numb rustle
of indigo silk, a train of fluttering things
collecting followers on the way in a movement
that pulls them past the street light, past the windows
of neighbors'—gowns float wide as invitations;

Newcomers spread the word & leave the exhausted
on the curb with the burned-out casings
of railyard flares, sparkling paper hats,
the iris gardener can no longer resist the park,
& the other groups, attracted & ignored divide again,
gain momentum, spilling over themselves
effusive as cool lava out onto night highways.

CHORUS, ON THE DAY BEFORE

It was the one secret no one wished to share,
the one that arrives tomorrow,
maybe in the mail delayed by the storm front.
The cat, swaying on a limb frantic
for coordination, what was expected,
the tenor, held up, waiting for traffic.

I see you in the mirror. You have been
watching like a witness, smiling, half
hidden behind the door. Isn't this what
you were trying to say? The bachelor accountant
in Los Angeles saving to preserve his head,
severed & kept cool for posterity
& the future miracles of medicine;
if only that promissory note
hadn't washed up on the shores of Lake Vibljiik.

Even as the chorus approaches
with one voice, in the style of the period
conversing informally, it was
the old topic of the storm discussed
in the lobby of the church,
which was what you meant, the expectation
of everything, the improbability of snow
on the waking face, that others are
actually able to talk about themselves,

to receive letters from parishioners abroad,
impressed by nearly everything imaginable,
this occasion of coordinates, a chorus
of systems that is for the moment,
or for this moment, acceptable.

UTILITY

Opposed. We are opposed
at every turn
or as say a favor is found
the neighbor who has suffered
a loss passes
through the trees of his yard.
It is the end of a run.
Blackbirds flutter up
mixed among doves.
We are off again.

Language will never mean again
what it means here:
grief in the drowning river,
the wet soil seeking words,
the weight of field workers,
those creatures of utility
unable to lift their heads
in the orchards sleeping

the sleep of St. Presence the Divine
between extremes, they say in turn
'I will do it once more—for you,'
a son or daughter, but it was all
for tedium, the daily certitudes
deep as organ tones, the security
of cells in the office place
or the plant, clear as an appointment

book, those white assignments
of the foundry, the life
of the always mediocre who rise
in restraint, in a schedule
that stretches itself between
night waves. My neighbor has another
wife, & walks through the trees
of his yard at noon.

FIREFLIES AT HARSEN'S ISLAND

The group and the group leader said the wind
would never come to this town or to this,
so it was up & down the seaboard
until it was dead, dead as the basin
of human opinion, dead as the port
of Ephesus, dead as the once sacred
society that would survive it all,
its bright flags flying over the purpose.

    Word went out. In the yellow oily smear
    of midsummer's most profuse sunflowers
    they came from every county in the state,
    took ferries, came as far as Ohio
    to join the local farm families even on foot
    from the bar in *Sans Souci* with their evening
    partners they came, with bus loads of seniors
    to gather in the fields for nightfall & fairy light.

It would never happen again, not like this,
& it did not happen, so they settled in
for their stay—the immediate signal:
the popular ode turning on itself
like a leaf, a dove's wing, the wind dipping
into the waters of old ports & clouds
like the colonnades of Smyrna shifting
to accommodate them, for those few

    who alerted others, altering them,
    blips like the shouts of city boys
    at summer camp into the dark meadows,
    the bending neon silos, the ballrooms
    with balconies of bright ideas,
    dithyramb of lantern-glow, cold sulphur
    spirals of nymphs performing in the shapes
    of their shapes, heads filled with divine objects,

one moved forward into the immense dark
as Zelios was led past the port & the last
sphere of influence, forsaking all others
on the journey of no return, the bold
voice exchanged for a dawn of ghosts,
they returned to Bar Harbor, Twin Rivers,
the one fawn-eyed farm boy with the fruit jar
lantern, & those seniors in their gilded buses.

NARCOTIC CARAFE

The city was an invention
organized to sustain
an idea of (a) life,

what it is what
it could become.

This city was arranged
with the certitude of the Midwest
then fitted tightly to a membrane
like bell glass—a futurist's model
of what cities should be
sometimes credible for its distance
& for its artificiality.

Dweller, speaking against the cement:

I never wanted this language,
it was unnecessary once
invisible & on that
I'd place my mouth.

MINOR FIGURES

To land

                                        once again among giants
with the composure of a feather in blind trust
the wedding photo of my parents was taken in a vestry
so the day began with the certainty of new cloth

& father who did not care for Masaccio
& refused to travel by air
stood innocent of the pillars filled with forty
years of Detroit factory whistles & steam
enough to melt summer streets

in the shadow of the square
against the church of Milan
an acrobat like a stunned frog flipped in midair
performs for admirers of window models
in winter coats who hold dusty bottles
of flower water, for those who could not know

    the shadow of the length of the tower
    is the exact length of all returnings

again the steel feather cuts the scar tissue,
runs down the seam of the church like a zipper
so the summer asphalt is heavy with anise.

From an aerial view the minutiae scutter
five miles below in their own culture,
the Congo or the forests of Lombardy—

in his desperate whisper as with cigarette stains mounting
the wallpaper, the elevator operator says 'Come marry me,
marry me,' all day long
sending up compartments of rattling coat hangers.

RACCOON FEEDING IN THE GOLD RUN DUMPSTERS

What actually occurred cannot be known,
not even for another language   before dawn

magpies rushed the parking lot
below my bedroom window, a council
disputing territory, food sources,
the morality of disequilibrium
on the metallic film of the asphalt
squawking through the unknown terror
which had the residents trapped inside
staring out the windows
for the duration of the neurological storm,
eternal funeral begun with the magpies
coming, a family of raccoons waddled
into the scene, out for gourmet dining,
bandits of the garbage heap, nosing around
through bottles and cans for chicken bones,
bits of pie crust, always chittering
as they do, I pulled myself to the deck,
pitched stones which made no difference,
they went on until dawn, woke my son
who moaned, & at this hour another subject
of the gene of dread, with the cantings of the magpies
& coons & my own unknown event
entered in my muddy notebook, the stones gone,
I returned to bed, the world resumed
its conference uncertain as I was
the wind picked up leaning into a forecast
of early showers among clouds.

SMOKE

One speaks

                              through the image

the image   maker

said   without a puff

                              of smoke,

every space has continuity, he added

                falling

                      to the quarry.

EXCERPTS FROM A REVIEW
 Prelude to a Poem

The following excerpts were taken from the galley sheets
provided by Jim Gove of Minotaur Press for this writer's review
of Bl( )ank Space, (Runaway Spoon Press,) by John Dolis.

The subject of language itself may become the most distinctive
trait (if not the distinguishing feature) of late-twentieth and early
twenty-first century poetry and the literature it stimulates. The
diversity of its application alone should do much to forward the
case. Beyond the grossly experimental—the most obvious
signature of our period—and from the early work of the 'modernists'
there has been an increasing emphasis on words themselves; on the
exact word and the multimorphemic nuances of the inexact, on polyphony
and *entendre,* and on the range and limits of language in the inevitable
journey into *medium-as-subject.*

   This emphasis has gathered momentum through the decades with
a vitality that has seized a stable share of the postmodern conscious-
ness . . . .in the heart of the living, the 'I' is the property of language,
a 'letter' and the ego is surrendered from the beginning . . . . the
conscious 'lettered' mind must be put aside, reconstructed, or on
other occasions, obliterated so communication may emerge with
the 'language' of the unconscious . . . . to become language itself,
the pure idea of (simultaneous) experience, requires an elemental
act which brings with it the sensation of absence, a white-out, a
blank space, as in "The Borghese Gardens," *The s( )n/ descends*
like a distance/ upon identity. There is in this dissolution, the
ambiguity of violence and delight.

   Once it is discovered that the individual persona has been made
mute, *The image comes apart/ at the seams, bleeds/ beyond the*
fabric of embodiment, ("Hawthorne",) when language becomes
the *prima materia* of reflectivity as it does here, the specter of
spiritual or aesthetic failure haunts every possible scene, revisits
every perception, a double of the conscience that cannot survive
the act of creation, a speechless image condemned to observe the
perpetual multiplication of other images which must issue
uncontrollably from it.

EXCERCISES IN HUMAN TAXIDERMY

for John Dolis

Reclining with a pocketful of lead anchors
on the faded ottoman with its stuffing pulled
out, you've caught them, the notions
at their dalliance from the fanlight
in the door of the Hotel of Paris
& mobile in the mountain haze,
the night air like an alcoholic mist
in a Colorado ghost town.

How you went on & on with them,
these figures, the notions, the masquerade,
each bulb of the chandelier a dull web,
each web a chime

that wouldn't do for one of the others,
a prominent member of a personality
stuffed into a bag, moved forward
with a receding hairline to proclaim
his own position pulling at the method,

a ranting military consultant in the court of the Medici,

'Is the Queen dead? Have we killed the Queen?
(for she was the source of our misery,) & her daughters,
persistent reminders, like sons, are apt to speak,
have you murdered them as well?

Pliny, when among the Caribs,

fixing them up so they looked good,
the ottoman worn at games as a cap or crown
would turn into itself & stands in evidence,
setting the tarsier right-side up:

is the object any less reasonable than the proposition?

With the acquisitions of our new properties,
erratic middle-age birthmarks,
unprotected from the results of ideas,
the creative murderers, courtiers dancing say
we have become an endangered species,
the endangered ones, we are the white men
do not forgive us our history,
you, old Europe, were of a mind,

& the faces were the same, bleached
like dried fruit, dolls pinched, stunned, the apple faces
of the athletes stranded in the Andés,
cracking the cases, blessing their friends,
cursing festivals . . . the flesh is sweet . . .

Expecting a moral passage we sat upright
to 'Autumn' from the Titanic,
a Roman holiday bringing the girl
& the trained donkey into the Colosseum,
adulation, & more relatives came . . .

Piazzi, you at once familiar in a crowd
fixing up the *Historia Naturalis* in a mercury vapor
counting you lobes
a mad balance between two mad extremes
suspecting heresy: the entire race in one body . . .

Tho' flesh is sweet they are drinking themselves to sleep,
& have come upon the stupor in which we came
upon them & by their posture offer more weight,
the hammock sagging with fruit
bending the saplings of the grove
& beyond, the road of kneecaps . . .

In the position between couriers
we are the subject of our trances . . .

& as we were fit for slumber
Alberich popped up, struck an obelus across the text,
put Doppler's eye under a glass hammer
& proclaimed: the retina is obsidian—

Honorably ungrateful for our deicides,
question, notions, & the rifts
left in the outback, you go on
expelling graphite calling cards
like a slot-machine, 'Daguerre, Daguerre,'
with a force (another Suspect)
that should by morning shatter the pane.

SONORA SAYING

Sonora

or what you are

saying

what you are not,

Sonora, your hills are mauve,

there is dried blood on your gown.

SOMETHING LEFT FOR OTHERS

You said everything I wanted to hear
maybe all that could be said at the time,
    the troubled boys in gangs going door to door,
    adolescent sweethearts showing up
from the party at midnight, tired, wandering
    off again, from the beginning, on the snowy

day we first met indoors, it was unavoidable
    as this conversation, and later
when we both moved it was difficult to keep
in touch, but you did all you were able to do,
    the glimpse between the passenger trains,
this much was clear, there was the presence

    of others, maybe you needed them here
as if it had become too much, like rates
    of interest, an unending mortgage,
    too much for you alone, the responsibility
of outsized landfills, the requirement of others
    to attend—you did all you were able to do.

URBAN DEVELOPMENT

The field is cleared, is cleared,
clear of trees torn up,
cleared of stumps blown out—

before we came to the explosions
with words that signify no object
the impact was realized
& is realized as the field is cleared
with the velocity that sent us off
in the convolutions of our means
as if they were equal to those
that surround us,
those that will invade us—

what builder would consider
the development as grounded
in the flash over the field?

& now, just as we are convinced
the field is contained
the edge dissolves toward us

SCIENCE FICTION

Arcosanti, Paolo Soleri's archology, a pedestrian-city seventy miles
north of Phoenix, Arizona, is designed to eliminate urban sprawl, blight,
and pollution. Composed of airy concrete cell-and-vault clusters to
suggest spiritual resonance and organic cohabitation with the desertscape,
the locals, and some architects of reputation, regard it as something
of a joke, a folly, akin to science fiction.

In a smoky subterranean complex,
the officials in their gray metallic uniforms
congratulate themselves on their recent victory.
The Forces of The Seventh Power
have been driven back to M 433, a tiny planet
in the far corner of another system in a remote nebulae.

& all of this without a single casualty,
due to the power of the new disequilibrium sensors,
now the Federation of The Pure
may once again turn its energy & attention
to its calling:

> shared transtemporal receptors
> infrasonic harmonies
> prolongevity portals
> ecocolonization
> painless passages between doubles
> holographic conveyances
> > (to make the incomplete whole)
> the conversion of nonsentient matter
> & the textilization of invisible garments
> > for the bodies of the pure

though none of this could pass the scrutiny
of those who reject the *genre*, which has become
a predictable reaction, reinforced by tradition,

not realistic enough, unconvincing, contrived,
not like human grief & suffering, blood in sand,
not like those chronic circles of tragedy
which must continue to turn & all who must
face the epic contests, always against
superior forces, what kills heart & soul.

SIX FANTASY LECTURES

The Iris Fields, Boulder

The police psychic stopping here
   nearing the fertile crescent
would only sense difference,

specters around the doctrine of the elect
   on the morning of the perfect ode,
the shadow-echo in spring,

an imitation in the bright
   silent deluge of small things
scrambling over walls & into other yards

admired by clairvoyants on gravel paths
   holding forth on factories
redolent with moral units, loam, production

schedules, the crimes of course were
   imaginary, forgiven as soon
as they went away, we never passed

the first introduction to the night's best
   notion, the night when the heart of hearts
goes wild, guardian & giver of direction.

THE CARMINE CYCLE

i

The firebirth of the female cochineal
extinguishes the water
moving like the pattern of a waltz.

ii

The limits of observation have forced
the diffusion of the question
in the pronoun of the cochineal
whose imperial theme is the color
that consumes the astronomer's clock
thrown out in the middle,
Wednesday walking into rainy Wednesday.

iii

Limitless they are, the limited
frames lining the lake,
a chenille panorama
where iron microbe & micron meet,
rust out another gender.

iv

This compression of gestures
mimes the miniature conch directing
the movement of a waltz
on a floor that is not flat,
learning the box step we practice variations
to dusty draperies, & the gray endless morning street
outside.

ORCHIDS OF CRETE

For those who have been too much
in the mind of things

lately, whenever they are
confronting themselves

like the thought of a world
collapsed to a line,

by way of it, a tissue
of another overlay, one

of multitudes, what arose,
moved forward, known

as we would know it,
the one thing that needed nothing

like a hidden segment
of dark matter behind

a cloud, matrices of white
& yellow cream

living in the mind of things
either for itself or for some

remote connector who comes
or who does not,

flung out, hidden
islands in the night sky.

SUNDAY PICNIC

A postscript: I saw the storm
   rise over the lake,
   you left the scene,
   walked off into the tall grasses blowing

which has led me to this:

if reason is white like the anger of the knuckle
   & desire drips valentine red
   spread like a tablecloth on the lawn
then all the signs & tissues of substance
   give every expression a form
   & every form its idea of expression,

as bubbles rise from fishes' mouths,

the world of water & the world of air
   melodic as grass or cloud or moving star,
   the great hatcheries of the night glitter with scales
like a tablecloth rippling in summer wind.

LINES ON A DOG'S FACE

Wallace said, 'What the eye beholds may be
the text of life,' & in this case it is
the Springer, Cynthia, whose eyes
are the brown corridors of vacuity,
moral deserts where the absolute Nothing
is, or nothing but her repetitions,
the fenceline patrol, the daily quarrels
with the cat, begging always for scraps
& a nap to sleep it off, then waiting
alert for something to be known.

Agent of operation, living primordium,
memoir of Something clearly in her stare
which would say only, 'I have know this
for a very long time,' retriever
of the stick locked in crocodile teeth,
living the life of the fanciful
scenario, chasing doves, the evening
meal, her wrinkles busily playing
out a program, a contemporary opinion,
the repetitions that govern her earth, & mine.

SECOND BEST

This category includes everyone
who hasn't finished first,
that is, most of us at one time
or another. Even when we win

the title, it is not forever,
eventually everyone forgets
everyone else, and the truly important
must live in their own hearts

while they are still beating.
There is some advantage to second place.
We are free to join the throng
of the anonymous drifting off

to the unknown where nothing is expected,
a consolation to be wished,
to recall ourselves
the desolate shore

covered with the detritus
of rocks in winter & what winter
left upon it, & the lake
all warm & heart-shaped now

with a pink sandy shore
& the trees—were there ever trees?
seen as through a golden gauze,
childhood's fondest autumn.

Here it is then: the mind sculpts
the past & what becomes
art—synaptic configurations
bent on the pathways of survival—

we call memory
recombining the old shoreline
to sift out degrees of better or best
like the rainforest canopy

that protects the subcortical structures,
ancient seats of anger & grief,
source of the primal howl
rising up through the limbus,

through epochs like electric waves,
blue & translucent
to pass for virtue & reason,
second best.

FLYLEAF

Nothing collapses so easily
in the fist than this,
the onion skin that crinkles
like the sound of the word, creation.

It is the twig that bows
in the wind & sweeps over the forearm,
or the peach that brushes
against the peach,

& these are found in pages
as if among a feathery crowd
of angels jostling in awe
toward the next wonder just ahead.

It is all the round syllables,
the talk of the world
trying to fill us with sense
again.

DOCTRINE OF COMPLICITY

We were never really alone in this,
call it our organic anthology.

Our acts & those of others recombine.
Take the three sisters—one called the other

who left the third alone in the apartment
& shortly thereafter suffered a stroke

which could have been prevented
by a physician of some reputation

who was, at the moment, unreachable,
pursuing a dalliance across town,

meanwhile the sisters under powder blue
parasols walk along one of the quays,

here, the accomplices, unknowing or not,
create the event. They are French.

In our togetherness anthology where we live
our condition is like this, inextricable

as the harvest workers prayer group,
or companies of paramilitary moving

in fields of complications
shaped by hands of horror, solace, *fait accompli*,

age of anxiety, age of doubt,
complicity leaves nothing out.

THE SUBLIME

The search for the sublime is central
to our condition, one we cannot resist,

one that should not be spoken of
directly & best left to experience

like Brunhilde in Fuseli's painting,
taken heart & soul with the image

of Gunther, suspended nude from a ceiling.
It is this. And more. Floating

embryonic life that is complete,
& thus, our attempts to recreate

other pathways—*inter vivos,*
the endorphins from jogging,

contemplation, Xtasy, Jameson.
These offer a temporary state only.

We need sublimity without end.
The record left by artists

offers some reassurance—this has been so,
it is an artificial life, one between, alone,

& cannot sustain what is in nature,
its best thought naked, alone.

The sublime is sacred
disequilibrium, or the notion of ascension,

even in this, even as we are moving
toward the inevitable

there is still a world
of sleeping human heads

resigned in *umbra mortis*,
shadows among shadows.

THE NATURE OF THINGS

The nature of things in midwinter
is clear. It is market day,
the refrigerator is empty, the engine
block, frozen, & it is two miles
to town. I set out in stocking cap
& woolen coat with collar up
through snow & wild winds.

I take a short cut through a wooded lot
& stop in a place of dwarfed trees,
brambles, balls of twigs that slow the sheets
of icy air that cut across everything.
The ground is gray,
hard & cold, down,
I am driven down, I know
I will accept anything
if it is warm.

EPISTEMOLOGY

There could have been other scenes as well
as these, by way of the flame or the forest,
or say, iris and calla lily, but the range was set,
the discursive mandalas of book clubs,
archologies, the long miles
of mental villages along the riverbanks
that are always changing—
what were we ever trying to make
of the waters' patterns and its confluences—
the doxology of the dream
to which we surrendered every ounce of belief
only to leave it for another
like an unfaithful lover
behind the scenes,
multiple courtships in the same house—
strangers to each other,
more visitors to the central library,

if only we had more time to read.

ELEMENTS OF INSTRUCTION

To be a victim requires communal understanding,
more or less, most must agree on the condition
of the underserved, a social state
of affairs. One is approved or not.

Before the accident no one paid attention,
but now they're paying.
It's history, like a series of collisions,
or a periodic table

and curiosities so odd
most agree they are worth recording,
& repeating to others

as if we were the ones
who gave up everything
for a moment, for memory,
like an ad,
like real estate.

HYMN TO CAPRICE

You were not everything, but nearly so, half
at least, attending the occasions often
the deciding factor, certainly the unexplained
grip of some early morning tension
and its sudden release returning us to ourselves,
moods that were a matter of public record—

The timing of teen suicides, or the case of spontaneous
combustion, the elderly aunt who left the family reunion early
and was consumed. Her remains found the next morning,
a ring, shoelace grommets, pelvic & cranial bone,
the mattress burned straight through. Another added variant
to the evening sky, erased, replaced with others tomorrow.

The extra aftershock at carnival through the streets of Rio,
the snake-dance at 3 a.m. and true to form there also
at the wheel as the family of seven swung
onto the wrong shoulder in the dust storm,
or our own impulse to pass in the clearest moment,
the rages of the road, shifts of climate solely

for the sake of spontaneity, the unnecessary
eruptions of the individual, the household, volcanic fields,
the one unnamed profile of a divine on a wall fountain
in ancient Hamartigenia that has baffled anthropologists,
for wantonness, prudence sulks & with faith composed
a motet for a dormant year, what is your defense,

an anodyne for monotony, or absence itself,
hummingbirds' throats the same dark color, the road
always reporting the same configuration, and if ever
you were part of a plan, you have stolen the show,
entrepreneur of the vogue, hair style and dress, affection too,
patron of the charge card, instant credit

and buyer's remorse, there when the workers' strike was called,
the militia sent, existing on the edges of things, in a margin
of error to take over the entire page in a flash,
history replaced by the embrace of the bright second
of certainty, to you we owe at least half of everything,
half our income and our longings,

our age, the conscious states from which reputations,
even lives are made, our first loves were determined
by as much, when they occurred, on what dark roads
and what was sought thereafter, prosperity, long life,
rectitude, citrus bloom, when to arrive,
return, or vanish in a blaze, reverie.

SALTON SEA

It is the purest body
of sensation, the heavy
liquid shrine of saline
& by all rights should have died
long ago & instead found
the essence of composition,
pale, complete, surrounded,
where bleached light & water join
blandness & a climate formed
a resting place for the winded
creatures of the Pacific
Flyway, Artic gulls & white
endangered pelicans, others
yet to be identified
bobbing on the warm water
below sea level, a place
of convalescence, vacant,
full of things that are
& are not wavering in the purest
forms imaginable.

WASHING BEFORE SEX

To complete what we begin
without interruption is a common desire,
but this cannot always be the case.
Even when listening to the purest
Aria, we understand the dog must be let out.

Smaller things do matter,
hygiene among them, a courtesy
to our partners. A century ago
once a week was considered sufficient,
but even this basic act must be made more
difficult, like so many others, like romance
itself, how many promises and minor luxury items
has it taken to get here, to this one moment

when a quick shower is required?
Washing before sex is a duty,
like moaning, call it homage to vanity,
if nothing else, or for reasons
that can be imagined. The Romans knew
this, the cult of tubs, the Baths of Caracalla
for example, full of sex and steamy politics,

or the adolescents eager for those summer trips
to the lake, cavorting for hours in the shallows
where the water bears weight and moving
the essentials is so much easier.
Affection for prolonged bathing has been reported
by partners attempting a sustained amniotic orgasm,
or fetal sex. The bodies of the dead are washed
for proper burial, and hands are scrubbed
after dove-gutting.

Washing afterward is a given
like the Clean Plate Club, or coming in
from gardening, or at the end
of the late night shift, a standard practice,
and once the afterglow cools,
what is wet, chills, until all that is left
is damp, a reminder of the necessity
of obligation, remorse, the aquatic life.

LEGACY OF GLANCES

What stuns the base of the brain,
hosts dead-heat, swamp rot, bogs
of human bones that bump with the weather,
is here also between the satellite dishes
on the pink tile roofs of the local tennis courts
of Oro Valley, or your own neighborhood,
among the green acrylic & the blue acrylic
surfaces, among the gardens
& the garden walkers,
clubby bronze sculptures that spout water
onto scalloped tiers that tip & tip again,
held by swans' wings, sea lions,
a monolith, surrounded by stiletto cypress,
the invisible clouds forming above the clouds
& always with the same attraction,
starting out new all over again,
lives without bodies, or an infantry;
formations of letters, these daytime elegies
in a glass atrium,
see-through receptacles,
a legacy of glances.

HOUSE OF CELESTIAL WONDER

The house of celestial wonder is located clearly
in the pop-up guidebook of cosmic affection,
along a stretch of Oceanside frontage & the peach orchard
wrapped in peach fog and the odor of peaches.

It was all made possible by the amusement park nearby,
garish & shrill, constructed by local prisoners
in the name of reformation,

& those sacred events that went through the roof
are now no less than a waterfall of blurry stars
sliding into musical streams
running down lanes of memory.

ORIGINAL MINDS

may not take expression from any living thing,
or dispute themselves or their own emanations
& cannot be found behind Wal-Mart, Intel,
or other big ideas & are, at the moment, locked away
busily working out a new script for themselves
in their alcoves of air
in the great hall of transcendence.

Original minds are not necessarily what we think
& may not produce artifacts as we know them,
besides themselves they are *a cappella*,
& may not understand human questions,
diagramming themselves as they do
in the explorer's moment, & known to perish in orphanages,
convent fires, rehab groups, & leave without leaving
a trace, some life complete from any outward sign

THE OBJECT & THE ADDRESS

Though it was morning & it was summer,
the morning after the party, there were judgments,
complaints from compromise, emphatic smudges
on the window & distortions of heat wavering
from the sill, the nude returned to the table
& to the objects on the table, to the letters & the bowl
asking for an exact duplication of carnival glass
or a description of the morning news,
sponsors & co-sponsors, themselves products
of the unending relationship & the burden of parentage,
such unprintable biographies have passed
between the object & the address,
the morning look, the blurred focus
over the orifice of an empty bowl
& the prospect of parity washing
& washing as if in air—

        film of film   memory of memory

what is the life of objects
in the process of impresence, in the flavored space
left after almond?

MORAL RAGE

Swirling. It's what students do
with the curriculum of their bodies,
spinning fractals, the charged catalogue
of the disformed, the corrigenda, The Earthly Book

& today I've had it
with the everything-that-is-part-something-else,
the dwarves of silence peeking through the fence,
tortoise's parrot-beak, papered hop-dry wisp
of dragonflywing, pyrolysitic vault,
thistle claw catfoot plant, elephantear,
cactus-phallus, head of oryx, heliosloth
& batwingmoth, the infant-fingered
tail of swampgorth & oracle beetle,
scaly locks, shardy teeth of calcareous thorn,
& dots of ord, parades overbanking
farmy lanes with wherefores
& wherefores, mixtures & co-mixtures,
vocal & sub-vocal, above & below,
to see clearly one transparent life form,
trying to pull the self a-part—to be one's self—
a single thing, sentenced in this mix & muddle.

INSOMNIA

As the sutures tighten
on the scalp along the incision line,
the surgeon explains, there will be
the sensation of scratching rats,
a phrase he assures me,
his patients remember,
I tell him I understand,
it is as if the rats
are trying to get at the ants
crawling around my brain.

He speaks to me a floating
observer, as if I had been roaming
about like an affection
or some other
misplaced condition.

It is 4:30 & I have been awake
since midnight in a soundless,
carpeted room, its furniture gone
as if the surgeon in his skill removed
the last remainder of mind,
until a neighbor who has risen early
for work coughs once
& begins again to scrape
the ice from his windshield
reminding me of what is human.

THE KISS

Among the trillion themes
of the natural universe, or its acts,
suction must be essential.

Planets, entire star systems
swallowed by black holes, the red
dust from the deserts of China
swirled up by global wind currents
& deposited on the peaks
of the French Alps, (a fact not
unnoticed by nuclear scientists,)
& all the suction that occurs

       in water vortices, down drafts,
       in gravity itself, tornado funnels
       that suck up homes, whole bodies,
       & the suction that goes on under stadium bleachers,
       in the back seats of cars & mini-vans,
       the true love of sexual contractions,
       biotubes, soda straws

& in the single act of a kiss, the kiss of the lover
or the spouse, the cosmic kiss, what pulls us inside
& is taken in

THE MATHEMATICS
OF ADORATION

The pink geranium reflected in the glass
of the patio table will never be
as intense as it is this moment
when it is perfect
as a ring of words
that has no counterpart beyond itself
as the flower is this moment a reflection
of itself, fire-pressed in glass & all
other things that are precisely now.

DEPARTURE

The other self, the one that speaks would say
I am seen only now as myself,
as I am leaving, over & over
again to all I have ever known,
to what makes leaving possible,
a practice, the letting go, to move without,
to move along the slopes of another
place where I remain more & more myself,
elevated and unexplained.

Note: *Departure was composed by invitation for the painting*
      of the same title by Laura den Hertog which appeared
      on the cover of 10 x 3, No. 3, Morgantown, WV, 2008.

SONG OF THE SOLAR FLARE

The essences that curl under heat
are dancing duets with words
& the throngs crossing
the Delaware, Rio Grande,
the black & brackish Irish Sea,
infant corps trodding over Africa
the legions of aviators crisscrossing
themselves spiraling upward & upward
intertwined with umbilicae & central
nervous systems, like invisible electric cords,
empty-headed escapades & the endless
spinnings of cavaliers.

SUMMER OCCUPATIONS

If the exchange is complete
it is returned as if to ask again—
the representative rubbing
of the bilingual self,
twin escorts with token transfers
on the Skyline Express
in anticipation of an evening,
the image of the tree in the heart,
or leaf-heart in the tree,
branch and *mons veneris*,
a claim, the taking in, like a review.

FIVE EPILOGUES

BURIAL GROUND

INDEX OF RENUNCIATIONS

For what was never known & still known,
what was teased away, taken, distracted
elsewhere, whorls of nightsteam assembled
in the unexpected, the unkept schedule
the next flitting combination
of trellis shadow & cloud shadow
& the winter branch across a white porch

diverted, for the thing that almost was,
that never reached the ledge of the language
of itself, for the extensions that floated
about a shape from lambent torsion sprung,
raided by other tensions, for movements
of the imagined, for the unseen lives
of their expressions

which go off without us, outside of the few
things of the conscious mind, for the always-
occurring to reveal some strand, tincture,
the copperpeach reflections on an evening
puddle, some patch or section for the poem
that attempted these things,
for its abode of longing,

the brick school in the wet morning,
for the act that concurs with every other act
of disclosure, for the life crisscrossed
with these, for the soul of one night
full of itself, requiring nothing,
for the perpetual cancellations of experience,
for their coilings,

unformed destinies winding through metal groves,
for the renunciations themselves,
for the fields of reported flowers,
suggestions half-made, caught, hand over mouth,
for the replacements, for what was found
least & most, inadequate, removed,
for all things then, for ourselves.

THE TROPIC GARDENS
OF ST. GALLEN

In memory
of Ezra Pound

Were done with old dreams
sagging like vines after winter

sinew-netted the ruins
Roman or Swiss crowd the mild day
subjects of impatience
spring, statues tighten
with passion flowers

like elongated hands
sought in the dark
approaching the gables
of disfigured hunters and porous fawns
above the pillars and the checked parquet
tiles of another setting the night brought
from its changing geometry

and we walked among them
as though to discover at last
what intricacy our walking would bring

to perform the great task
we imagined perfection
so we would always seek it

the gardens of language

and turned away toil spent
like the widow's silk on the cornices at Tivoli
or the willows of Chapultepec,

companion, talking with your hands
under the dry trellis
in your winter blanket and mountain chair,
you have been faithful to the world

to the gables
the Alpine gables

BEST SAID

Some things are best left unsaid,
  the long-term promises of lovers,
  the life one wished one would have led.

Other things are better left unread,
  tomorrow's obituary, the bad review,
  the things about us others said.

Some things are better left undone,
  the great project that could never be,
  misunderstood by nearly everyone.

Some things are better left with the dead,
  so much of what is best said
  dies with its owners, unloved, unread.

PREGNANT GIRL ON THE GENESEE
RIVER BRIDGE

I have taken a bench on the bridge
my parents walked when courting
under the shadow of the Times-Square
building in downtown Rochester.

The city scene is gray, intentional, a mini-Gotham,
the waters of the Genesee slow & dirty-green,
shallow & fetid, where I've come out
once again to greet the evening.

And she appears, a child herself
carrying another under the faded rainbow
tank-top stretched tight & stained, she leans
against the heavy railing and stares at the water.

High above the white gulls fly
toward the great lake. They use the river
as a guide, like a line on an aerial map,
& the child smiles at me, once, turns away & sighs.

What is here is here & what has gone has gone.
Under the steel towers, under the statue of Mercury,
the brick & glass looming over the bridge,
such ruins among such strong forms.

THE PINK STUCCO HOUSE
ON ST. MICHAEL'S STREET

All you ever left behind meant nothing.

It has come to this, once again,
the ingenious solo, the renovated
house, albums of the old family, the one
classic theory, the book, the immaculate shop.

These are now the memories of a process
(that belong to someone else) & not the process,
not even the letter you wrote yourself (an entry)
to reconstruct it all. This too was nothing

when compared to the pitch of the sidewalk
near the ocean on the one morning when you watched
yourself among others, or alone visiting
the pink stucco house on St. Michael's Street.

Made in the USA
San Bernardino, CA
14 November 2015